There is Hope

There is Hope

A strategy to reach your world for Christ

For Visionaries Only

Leo Habets

Marshall
Pickering

Marshall Morgan and Scott
1 Beggarwood Lane, Basingstoke,
Hants RG23 7LP, UK

First published in 1988 by
Marshall Morgan and Scott Publications Ltd.
Part of the Marshall Pickering Holdings Group
A subsidiary of the Zondervan Corporation

ISBN: 0 551 01759 7

Text set in Baskerville by The Ikthos Studios,
Chute Forest, Andover, Hampshire.

Printed in Great Britain by Cox and Wyman,
Reading

Contents

With much gratitude to Jose Monells, Markku Happonen, Hanspeter Nüesch, Myles Wilson and David Hill for their contributions to this book, and to Annette Wiltink, Sheila Barter and Linda Anderson for typing and editing the manuscript.

INTRODUCTION

The Challenge is Yours

Dear visionary,

There are 350 million people living in Western Europe.

The vast majority of these people 'exist' without knowing God. Millions of people around us live and die without the Lord Jesus Christ. They literally are like sheep without a shepherd, harassed, helpless and ultimately with no hope.

There are 24 nations in Western Europe. Most, if not all, of these societies have turned away from God. Because of that, we can see our continent shrouded in spiritual darkness, resulting in all kinds of sins and problems. 'Where there is ignorance of God, the people run wild.' (Proverbs 29: 18, *Living Bible*)

But in Europe there remains a small 'remnant' of people who have a living relationship with God. And since you have picked up this book I take it that you belong to this minority.

We Christians are the ambassadors of the Lord Jesus Christ among people who are living without God and in societies that have turned away from their Creator. We have been entrusted with the good news. We should be the ones who distribute the life-giving hope that Jesus Christ has to offer to all 350 million of our fellow Western Europeans in all 24 of their nations.

We are the light of this continent; the salt of

Europe. If not through us, then how will people in Western Europe ever hear the message of hope? 'How then, can they call on the One they have not believed in? And how can they believe in the One of whom they have not heard? And how can they hear without someone preaching to them?' (Romans 10: 14)

I have written this book to encourage and motivate you to take the initiative in sharing Jesus' message of hope with the people around you. I also suggest a strategy for proclaiming the good news to all the people in your neighbourhood, village, town, city, region, or even your whole country. If we Christians all stand in our own 'Jerusalem' and take responsibility for a tiny part of this vast continent, God will shine out through us into the darkness of Western Europe. Those 350 million people have the right to hear. We have the privilege and responsibility to tell.

This book is a personal challenge to YOU. Read it; pray and think about your role as an ambassador of the Lord Jesus Christ and dream great dreams for your society. Dream dreams that only God can fulfil. Let Him use you for His glory.

May God bless you richly — and many others through you.

There is hope.

Leo Habets

Chapter 1

We dare not be silent

In II Kings, chapters 6 and 7, we read an interesting story. King Benhadad, the ruler of Syria, had mustered his entire army and attacked the city of Samaria. But the city was stronger than he expected. He could not conquer this rich fortress. So the king and his troops besieged the city.

For a long time his troops camped around Samaria. No one could get in or out. More importantly, the supply of food to the city was completely cut off. Eventually their food reserves were completely exhausted. The Samaritans had nothing left to eat.

Rather than starve, they started to eat anything they could find — even heads of donkeys and doves' droppings. Not only that, they were willing to pay a lot of money for this food that was not real food at all! Some of the citizens became so desperately hungry that they ate their own children.

Outside the city were four lepers. They lived in no man's land, camped between the city and the enemy. Now, if the situation in the city was bleak, the situation in this no man's land must have been ten times worse. After some time the four lepers reasoned: 'If we stay here we will surely die. Going back to the city is impossible, because they will not let us in. And even if they do let us in, it will not help us because there is no food left in the city. The only chance we have to survive is to go to the camp of the enemy and surrender to the army of the Syrians. They will probably kill us, but we will die here too.'

That evening the four lepers set out towards the Syrian camp. With the courage of those who have no hope and nothing to lose, they were ready to surrender to the Syrian army.

As they approached the camp, everything was pitch dark and very quiet. The four men could not believe what they discovered. The impossible had happened: the army camp was completely deserted. The soldiers had gone leaving everything behind: tents, horses, silver and gold, clothes, weapons . . . and food. Lots of food.

Unknown to the hapless, broken lepers, the Lord had earlier created a terrifying sound of a huge army, with galloping horses and the clatter of speeding chariots. Believing that the Israelites were attacking, the Syrian army turned tail and ran for their lives.

It's not hard to picture the next scene. The four lepers headed for the nearest tent and ate, drank and pilfered their way through its contents. They went into another tent and did the same. Then into the next tent . . . and so on, until they could eat and drink no more. They carried off the gold and silver and hid it nearby to collect later. These four outcasts now had everything: they were well fed after months of famine, and they were rich after years of poverty. They had crossed over from hell into heaven.

But then something strange and beautiful happened. In the midst of the biggest party of their lives the four lepers suddenly looked at each other. 'We're not doing right,' they said.

'This is a day of good news and we are keeping it to ourselves. If we wait until daylight, punishment will overtake us. Let's go at once and report this to the royal palace.'

The four men had started to feel guilty that they were not sharing their amazing discovery with any of the starving people in the city. So back they rushed to the city to proclaim the good news to the starving citizens.

And what happened? The Samaritans refused to believe them. They suspected it was a Syrian plot to lure them out of the safety of the city walls. The four lepers had a message of life, but the dying people in the city would not believe them. They had a message of hope, but the people who so desperately needed hope thought it was a dirty trick.

Try to imagine how those four lepers must have felt. They must have pleaded with the people in the city. They probably showed them food and riches. Finally the king, having no other resource, decided in desperation to send out scouts to check the lepers' story. Two chariots were despatched. They went to the Syrians' camp and followed a trail of clothing and equipment thrown away by the army in their haste to flee from the invisible army of God. There was no sign of the enemy anywhere. The lepers' story was true.

The city gates were opened and the people poured out to plunder the deserted enemy camp. Suddenly there was enough food for all of them — food that represented life. There were weapons that provided protection, and there were riches that allowed for a more abundant life.

Suddenly there was hope for Samaria. A new future dawned: a new life started. And the four lepers are never mentioned again.

Spiritual donkey heads

This story provides a beautifully drawn picture of our own situation. We, too, live in a city, a country, a world where people are hungry. There is a spiritual starvation going on all around us in the lives of colleagues, friends, neighbours, even families. And because they do not know that real spiritual food exists, much less where they can find it, they are eating spiritual food which is not the real thing. Millions of people are eating spiritual donkey heads and doves' droppings. And, like the people of Samaria, many of them are paying hugely inflated prices for this phoney food.

Think of all the cults, modern theology, humanism, materialism, demon worship, the use of horoscopes, the popularity of mediums and spiritualists, and so on. The tragedy is that not only does this 'food' fail to feed them, but it also defiles them. Instead of bringing health to their souls, it brings sickness.

We Christians are like the four lepers. Once, we too were starving, but we went in search of real food. We discovered that the enemy has been overcome and that there is spiritual food in abundance. The time must now come when we too, look at one another and say: 'What we are doing is not right. This is wonderful news, but we are not sharing it with others.'

There is nothing wrong with eating all the spiritual food we can get, whether it is from the Bible, sermons, Christian conferences or books and tapes. But the spiritual food the Lord gives us is never for us alone. It is meant to be shared. We need to pass the food on to the starving

14

people. We must go back to the city, the country, the world to share the good news of what we have found. We must tell the people around us that they don't have to starve; that they don't have to eat food which is false. We have the good news that they no longer need to eat spiritual donkeys heads or doves' droppings, but that there is real life-giving food in abundance. We have to tell the people of our 'city' that their enemy has been overthrown.

Some people will listen to this proclamation of life and hope. They will join us and live. Others will not listen. They will not believe us. They will think that it is a lie, a dirty trick. They will laugh at us, but they will starve and die in their laughter.

Whether they listen or not, we Christians dare not be silent. We are the trustees of the good news, of a message of hope. We need to share it with the people around us.

An 'impossible' task

The Lord Jesus Christ told his disciples: 'All authority in heaven and on earth has been given to Me. Therefore go and make disciples of all nations, baptizing them in the name of the Father and of the Son and of the Holy Spirit, and teaching them to obey everything I have commanded you. And surely I am with you always, to the very end of the age.' (Matthew 28:18-20)

That is the Great Commission the Lord Jesus Christ has given us.

It is the greatest commission ever given to mankind. It is a commission for all Christians of all time, of all ages, of all countries and of all denominations. It is a commission that we

Christians have to take seriously for a number of reasons.

The love factor

First, we need to take the Great Commission seriously out of love for the Lord. Almost 2,000 years ago, Jesus Christ died on the cross of Calvary in our place. He paid the price for our sins. He set us free. He gave us hope. He bought us with His own blood and now He owns us. We belong to Him. He is our Master.

And our Master very clearly tells us to go, to take the initiative in sharing the good news. Frankly, we cannot call ourselves His followers if we are not willing to obey His commands. Our relationship with Him will suffer if we are not obedient.

And yet we should not share the good news only out of obedience. There has to be another factor. In Jesus' words: 'Whoever accepts My commands and obeys them, he is the one who loves Me. If anyone loves Me, he will obey My teaching. He who does not love Me will not obey My teaching.' (John 14:21,23,24)

There is, in fact, a direct relationship between love and obedience. If we love someone it is easy to be obedient. And if we are obedient it shows our love. But if we are not obedient, the reality of our love comes into question.

If we really love the Lord Jesus, we will find ourselves longing more and more to be obedient — and that means, among other things, being involved in some way in sharing the good news. That does not necessarily mean it will be easy — in fact Jesus promised us just the opposite! It simply means we do it because Jesus asked us to.

In the introduction I quoted Romans 10:14

'How, then, can they call on the One they have not believed in? And how can they believe in the One of whom they have not heard? And how can they hear without someone preaching to them?' But look at how the apostle Paul continues: 'and how can they preach unless they are sent?'

Well, as Christians we are all 'sent'. The Great Commission is for every child of God. As soon as we enter into a living relationship with the Lord Jesus Christ, the commission and the privilege of sharing the good news applies to us too. We can then gladly participate in the sharing of the most glorious message of hope ever. 'How beautiful on the mountains are the feet of those who bring good news!'. (Isaiah 52:7)

The starving billions

Secondly, we need to take the Great Commission seriously because people are lost without Jesus Christ. Jesus said: 'I am the way and the truth and the life. No-one comes to the Father except through Me.' (John 14:6)

Likewise, the apostle Peter told the Jewish religious leaders questioning him: 'Salvation is found in no-one else, for there is no other name under heaven given among men by which we must be saved.' (Acts 4:12)

That is plain language. We need to ask ourselves how that fits in with our own faith. Do we really believe that people are lost without Jesus Christ? And if so, what is our response to that? Do we love the people around us enough to tell them about Jesus?

Billions of people are starving because they don't have the only true spiritual food. These people will be lost forever if we don't share the

17

good news with them.

Hungry for God

Thirdly, we need to take the Great Commission seriously because people are hungry for God. Jesus said: 'The harvest is plentiful, but the workers are few.' (Matthew 9:37) Yes, the harvest is plentiful. People all over the world — and that includes Europe — are seeking spiritual answers, just as we once did. That people are not interested in God is one of Satan's favourite lies. He has a vested interest in making us believe that lie; for if we do our evangelistic efforts will decrease or even stop completely. Don't fall for it!

Pascal, the French philosopher and scientist, once said that there is a God-shaped vacuum in the soul of every human being that only God can fill. Many people experience this vacuum in a very real way. They may express it differently, but the pain, the emptiness of life, the longing for real answers are still there. Countless people are 'homesick' for God without realizing it, and without ever having met Him.

Well, we know Him. We are His ambassadors in this world, His representatives in the kingdom of the enemy. We know that the enemy has been overpowered. We know that the ultimate victory has already been won by Jesus Christ. We know that He wants to release people from the bondage of hopelessness. We know that in Jesus there is spiritual food in abundance. Therefore we need to share the Gospel and its message of hope for everyone, everywhere.

Finally, we need to take the Great Commission seriously because it is the only hope for our society. Most Western countries have turned away from God. As a result, many of them have entered into a great spiritual darkness, as I will explain more fully in the next chapter. I firmly believe that the only hope for these countries is to turn back to God. There is hope for our countries, for Europe and for the world if we start to acknowledge Him again and once more start to worship Him.

Christians need to take the Great Commission seriously, even though it may seem an impossible task to 'make disciples' of our own country and of all the other nations of the world. Let's face it — humanly speaking, the fulfilment of the Great Commission is far beyond our capacity. It is an impossible task. But there is hope. Look at the words the Lord Jesus added to the commission to go and make disciples of all the nations: 'Surely I am with you always, to the very end of the age.' He underlined the need for dependence on Him and the Holy Spirit with His last words here on earth before returning to the Father: 'You will receive power when the Holy Spirit comes on you; and you will be My witnesses in Jerusalem, and in all Judea and Samaria, and to the ends of the earth.' (Acts 1:8)

As we take the Great Commission seriously, the Lord Jesus will be with us everywhere and at all times. As we seek to share the message of hope, the Holy Spirit will give us power to do the impossible. God will do things in and through our lives about which we could not even begin to dream. Are you ready for this 'impossible' adventure?

Chapter 2

No hope generation

In what way does Europe resemble the Old Testament city of Samaria? Well, not least of all in the abundant life of the city. Europe has a very rich history and heritage. For many centuries this continent dominated the world geographically, economically, culturally and spiritually. Most autonomous European states had, until recently, their own colonies. About half of the world was at one time under the direct control of European governments. This power and influence brought with it economic prosperity, and many centuries the riches of the world were brought to our shores from the furthest corners of the earth. Europe blossomed into an abundant cultural centre. A fantastic variety of painters, composers, philosophers, writers and theologians emerged. Spiritually, Europe played the main international role. As well as the influence of the theologians, the Gospel itself was taken to many overseas countries by Europeans. In every sphere of life, Europe was at the centre of the world.

Under seige

That situation has changed dramatically. Two world wars marked the beginning of a complete shift in Europe's proud role in the world. Her

21

absolute power was soon lost to the United States of America and the Soviet Union, with China holding a strong third. In just one decade, European countries lost almost all of their colonies. Closer to home, some parts of Europe fell into Communist hands.

At the same time, birth control and economic pressures resulted in the population growth falling far behind that of other continents. In 1900 about 27 per cent of the world population lived in Europe. By 1980 that figure had dropped to about 15 per cent. By the year 2000 it is expected to be less than 10 per cent. Added to this is the fact that the average age of Europeans is getting older. Most countries are failing to reach the average figure of 2.1 children for every woman, which is necessary to keep the population at the same level. The result is a growing force of older people. As their numbers increase, so too their influence and power will grow; they are the future leaders of Europe.

In just one century, Europe will have changed from a unique world power owning half the entire globe, into a rich and comfortable old people's home representing less than a tenth of the world's population. This sudden change of direction has had, and will continue to have, a dramatic effect on the continent, the individual countries and the people. It affects the way we view life, especially our future. It affects our security, creativity, inner strength and attitudes. It influences our view of authority and, ultimately, our view of God. Europeans are under siege and it looks as if we are losing the battle.

Hunger in the city

Now for a quick tour through the 'city' of

Europe. What do we see?

At first glance life looks good. There is the beauty of a huge variety of landscapes from the majestic mountains of the Alps to the lowlands of the Nordic countries. Then there is the rich history evident all around: in the dynamic cities, in the ancient buildings, and in the mystical traditions. Life is colourful, and this finds expression in the arts. There are theatres, concert halls and museums all over the continent.

But far more important than all this beauty in nature, history and the arts is the fact that the people of Western Europe enjoy freedom. They can say and write whatever they wish. They are free to express their dreams, even their discontent, in almost any way they choose. All of Western Europe's countries have democratically elected governments; power lies in the hands of the common people. On the whole, they seem to rule this continent pretty well. Over an unpredecented 40-year period there has not been one war in Western Europe. Countries which have often gone to war with each other now live in peace. There is a growing unity between the different nations.

Economically too, Europe is still doing well. The standard of living is generally high. Social security is available. Educational standards in Europe are high. Medical science has reached incredible levels.

At first glance Europe appears to be prospering. It looks like a free and balanced society. But upon a closer look, how does Europe's heart beat? Are the 350 million people living in Western Europe happy and fulfilled? Do they feel secure and safe? Do they have faith in the future?

Let me try to answer those questions with

some revealing facts. Of the ten countries in the world that rank highest in suicide, eight are European. An EEC committee for medical research estimated that every year 1.4 million suicide attempts were made in the ten countries which formed the Common Market at that time. It was also estimated that about five percent of the total population (17.5 million people) tried at least once to kill themselves.

Even more alarming is the epedemic growth of suicide among young people. It has tripled in the last thirty years. In some countries, suicide ranks third as a cause of death among young people, behind only traffic accidents and cancer. Juvenile suicide is without question one of the most dramatic and worrying signs of the lack of spiritual stability and strength in Europe today. Is it coincidence that a spiralling suicide rate among young Europeans has occurred over the same period as a startling increase in the number of broken marriages? During the last twenty years, the number of divorces has increased by more than 500 per cent. In some countries there are now more divorces than marriages! At the end of this century it may well be that one in three European marriages is ending in divorce, leaving millions of broken homes. Innumerable young people are growing up without the security of a loving home, resulting in all kinds of other problems. Divorce is therefore a multiplier of social instability.

Another revealing sign of the emptiness of European hearts is their enslavement to drugs and alcohol. Many people, either bored by the status quo or looking for an escape from the harsh reality of life, turn to drink or drugs. One of the embarrasing facts about the decline of moral and social values in Western Europe is

24

that, in total, we spend more money on alcohol than on basic foodstuffs.

And alcohol and drugs create their own problems: road accidents, broken homes, prostitution, crime, causing an untold toll of human misery.

All over Europe we are seeing an epidemic growth in violence, rape, vandalism, child abuse and murder. Added to that are the frequent kidnappings in the name of revolutionary causes, the political massacres, the violent clashes between different groups in society, and the terrorist attacks on capitalist society. In West Germany alone, 1985 saw 1,604 violent political attacks, resulting in, among other things, a repair bill of 35 million German Marks for the damage done to public property. Most Western European nations now have their own extreme right- or left-wing terrorist groups: the Red Army Faction in Germany; the IRA and INLA in Britain; ETA and Grapo in Spain; the Red Brigades in Italy; the Communist cells in Belgium; Action Directe and the FLNC in France; and the FP-25A in Portugal. The media gives us detailed, full colour reports of their brutal work all over Europe. We and our children have become so familiar with these bloody reports that we accept them as a reprehensible but normal part of life.

Then there is the life-threatening problem of pollution. The sewage waste of 350 million people in our 'city' flows daily into our rivers, lakes and seas. Industrial waste is pumped in enormous quantities into our waters and the air. Millions and millions of cars pollute the air we breathe. Fertilizers used in the quest for higher crops are poisoning the soil. Europe no longer has a healthy environment. Trees and plants, of vital importance to the whole cycle of life, are dying. Many beautiful and historical buildings are deteriorating because of the pollution in the air. The ancient buildings in the city of Rome have been damaged more in the last 25 years than in the preceding 2,000 years.

If the buildings are being affected, it stands to reason that our bodies, too, will be damaged. Millions of Europeans suffer ill health and even die a premature death because of pollution. It is estimated that up to 80 per cent of all cancers and heart diseases are caused by pollution, and that soon one in four people in the more developed countries will have cancer.

Added to these problems are the growing fears about nuclear waste and the safety of nuclear power, and, worse still, a nuclear war. The Chernobyl accident not only polluted the air, the waters and the land of Europe; it also altered our thinking and greatly increased our fears for the future.

AIDS now occupies a similar position in public fears. It is estimated that the number of victims of this deadly modern disease — spread mainly by extra-marital sexual relationships and drug users' shared syringes — doubles every ten months. Because there is no cure yet available, people all over Europe (and the world) panic at the epidemic proportions of this slow killer. Some experts claim that AIDS is a greater threat to mankind than a nuclear war.

Of course I could go on and on like this. Page after page could be filled with disturbing facts about pornography, abortion, re-armament, unemployment, poverty, energy shortages ahead, materialism, euthanasia, huge national debts, rebellion against authority, depression, and so on.

All these problems and frustrations and fears have caused a great spiritual hunger all over Europe. The harvest is indeed plentiful, but because the workers seem to be in such short supply, millions of people are seeking answers in the wrong direction. They are eating spiritual donkey heads because they do not know that there is real spiritual food in abundance.

The United Kingdom is witnessing the greatest boom of occultism since the beginning of this century. In the Netherlands, a recent survey showed that about 50 per cent of the population believe in occult forces. In the same country another survey showed that only one in three people still believe in a personal God. In Kiel, West Germany, a national occult centre has been established. All over Europe, people are desperately seeking answers in astrology, hypnosis, magic and Eastern religions.

Yes, Europe's prosperity and happiness is only skin deep. Her heart is sick with emptiness, insecurity, fear and pessimism. The future doesn't hold many promises. For many Western Europeans, life is without hope. But no society can survive without hope. Everybody needs hope, something to believe in, to live for.

Who is offering this hope to Europe?

Where are the lepers?

There are over 350 million people in Western Europe.

More than 58 per cent of the population belong to the Roman Catholic church. About 17 per cent are members of one of the many Protestant churches. A small 3 per cent belong to the Greek Orthodox church. This means that 78 per cent of all the people in Western Europe *officially* belong to a Christian church.

There are thousands of churches all over Europe. It is hard to find one village, let alone a city, without at least one church. Then there are the many Christian institutes: universities, schools, hospitals, and a variety of social groups and organizations. But does all of this make Europe a Christian continent? Are the Christians in Europe effectively sharing the good news with a society that desperately needs it? Are the churches offering hope to the millions of Europeans who live in despair? The answer has to be a loud and clear 'No'.

Most churches are empty. They are religious monuments to past spiritual life. The church in Europe has lost its impact on society. In reality, the church in Europe is dying.

If you feel that this statement is too harsh, let the statistics speak for themselves. On a normal Sunday only three to five per cent of the European population (about 17 million people) attend church. By itself, that number may look impressive, but it also means that 95 per cent — that is 333 million people — are not in a church on that same Sunday. Of course, this does not necessarily mean that all these people do not have a living relationship with God, but neither does it mean that the small remnant who do still go to church really walk with the Lord.

The fact is that the spiritual bankruptcy of Europe is alarming. Millions of people have left the church and are no longer attracted to Christianity and the church as they see it.

Kalevi Lehtinen, an international European evangelist, sums up the situation: 'For the African and the Asian, the Gospel is good news. For the average European it is neither good, nor is it news. He thinks Christianity has been tried here, but did not work.'

I believe there is a lot of truth in that statement. Millions of Europeans — including most nominal Christians — have erected their own statue of Christianity based on their own experience and perception of it. But because they did not like what they saw, they have torn down their own statue. They want no involvement with Christianity as they perceive it to be.

All those Europeans have written off something they don't really know anything about. They don't realise that the enemy has been conquered. They cannot believe that the Gospel of our Lord Jesus Christ offers real hope, and that there is abundant spiritual food there for the taking. So they continue to eat spiritual donkey heads and doves' droppings. Instead of eating the living bread, they are starving to death.

To my mind this is the greatest drama being played out in Europe today. Stage left we see a church that is impotent and dying and does not have a message for the people in need. Stage right we have the millions of people who have turned away from their only hope, rejecting the message of Christianity as irrelevant.

A little flock

How many people in Western Europe are real followers of the Lord Jesus Christ, and want to be active as ambassadors of God on this continent?

Five million?

Maybe one million?

Only God knows.

But compared to the total population of Western Europe, it is only a very small minority. A small army of dedicated Christians scattered

29

throughout a continent that has turned away from God *en masse*.

The question is, who will influence who?

Will the secularized majority continue to influence the little flock that is left on this continent in such a way that it will continue to grow smaller and weaker? Or, as a little bit of salt enhances the taste of the entire meal, will this little flock influence the vast number of people in Western Europe?

Does the fact that Christianity in Western Europe has lost so much ground in a short period of time mean that the little flock of dedicated Christians has no role to play anymore?

Of course not!

On the contrary!

God delights to work through small groups of weak but dependent people.

In the example of Samaria only four sick lepers were used to bring the hopeful message of deliverance to the whole city. Gideon, by God's choice, had only 300 warriors left to conquer the mighty army of the Midianites.

Jonathan and his body-guard attacked the immense army of Philistines after he had said: 'Perhaps the Lord will do a miracle for us. For it makes no difference to him how many enemy troops there are.' (I Samuel 14:6. *Living Bible*)

The young David fought the great champion Goliath, who was about three metres tall.

King Jehoshaphat placed singers at the head of his army to praise God, after the prophet Jahaziel had told him: 'Do not be afraid or discouraged . . . the battle is not yours, but God's.'

Yes, it is a true saying of the apostle Paul:'When I am weak, then I am strong'. (2 Corinthians 12:10b) It is through our weakness that God can do His work and glorify Himself.

We committed, born-again Christians, a little flock on this continent, are the salt of Western Europe. Only a little salt is needed to make the food tasty. A few dedicated Christians are all that is needed to influence this continent for Jesus Christ. Only a few lepers are needed who are willing to step out in faith and trust God for the impossible.

The question is: 'Will you be one of them?'

Chapter 3

Visions are born

It was December 1977. I drove through the flat, cold and foggy northern countryside to a small old farmhouse. I and seven leaders of Campus Crusade for Christ's ministry in the Netherlands had decided to hide away for a few days to seek the Lord and to discuss the future of our ministry.

That retreat was to mark a new beginning in our work. For during our time at the farmhouse, the experience of those lepers thousands of years earlier was to become real for us, too. As the meetings went on, we became more and more burdened with the declining spiritual situation in our country and with the fact that millions of people around us were living and dying without Jesus Christ.

At the same time, we experienced a fresh gratitude for the new life God had given us through the death and resurrection of the Lord Jesus Christ. We knew we had been saved from certain death, but we also knew the scope of the spiritual starvation that surrounded us. Like the four lepers we realized, with a new clarity and urgency, that we needed to share the good news with more people than we had ever done before. Of course we had witnessed to many individuals, but it dawned on us that we had never proclaimed the most wonderful news ever to the whole 'city'

— in our case the whole of the Netherlands.

Like those four lepers we looked at each other and expressed this vision in their words: 'This is wonderful news and we need to share it with all the people.'

As we continued to talk and pray, God began to put such an amazing idea in our hearts that, at first, we didn't dare mention it to one another. But as the retreat went on we became more and more open with each other and it became evident that God really was trying to get through to us. He had a special plan for this retreat and this small group of young Christian leaders. Step by step God made it clear to us that He wanted us to be involved in proclaiming the good news to the whole country. His plan was made even more specific than that. We felt God was saying that our goal should be to bring the good news to all 14 million people living in the Netherlands before the end of 1985. That gave us eight years.

I remember very clearly our first reaction when we finally realized what God wanted us to do. We began to protest! 'Lord, this is impossible.''This job is too big for us.' 'There are only a few of us and we are all young.''We can never do this.'But then, in a moment of great holiness, we were overwhelmed with the presence of the Lord. We all knelt to worship Him. We praised and thanked Him. There were tears, there was joy, and there were fears. On our knees we re-dedicated ourselves to our Lord Jesus Christ and we pledged our lives to the spreading of the good news to our whole country. We dedicated our lives and our ministry not just to reaching individuals for Jesus Christ, but to sharing His message of hope with the entire nation.

After this time of praise, prayer and dedication, we tried to continue our meeting, but we had no idea what to do or even where to start. After all, how do you plan to get through to 14 million people with the Gospel? How could we get into every home in the country? And where would we find the money to do it? Hundreds of questions and absolutely no answers. The goal was clear, but we were completely without a clue when it came to working out how to accomplish our overwhelming, audacious task.

So it was with a strange feeling of insecurity that we left that farmhouse. I remember feeling one moment as if I was floating on cloud nine because of what God had done among us, but the next moment feeling like crying and hiding in the nearest hole because of the sheer impossibility of the vision He had entrusted to us.

When we left the farmhouse we were so uncertain about how we should handle our dream that we decided not to mention it to anyone — except our partners — for the next two months. For all those weeks, we hid this fantastic vision in our hearts. We prayed about it, wrestled with it, dreamed about it, but did not talk about it to anyone.

Then the same group of leaders got back together. It was another day I will never forget. During our meeting I asked the rest of the group: 'Do you believe, after all these weeks, that this vision is from the Lord? Do you still believe that this is what we should do and live for?'

One by one, the whole circle of leaders spoke. And one after another told of their hopes, fears and dreams. But seven times the answer came back: 'Yes, I believe this is from the Lord. We should do it.'

The project was on; the challenge accepted; the task begun. There was only one problem. We still had no idea how to do it.

This new vision and our reaffirmed dedication immediately started to affect our lives and our ministry. From then on we evaluated everything we did by the goal of proclaiming the Gospel to 14 million people before the end of 1985, and the Lord blessed us in a tremendous way.

Our staff more than trebled from 25 to 85. Eight lay training centres were started to help Christians learn to share their faith and to disciple others. Our organisation became involved in setting up a modern conference centre to provide year-round training for Christians. Hundreds of courses for church members were organised. City-wide evangelistic campaigns were held in several places. We started to publish a Christian paper that soon had a circulation of 30,000 copies every month.

Through all these efforts, the Gospel went out to many people, and thousands of Christians were built up in their faith. Many exciting things happened, but we were still not making any impact on the country as a whole. We were still not sharing the good news of real spiritual food with all our countrymen.

Then, in January 1980, I went to a Christian leadership conference in Spain. There I heard reports of what God was doing throughout Europe. These 'war stories' impressed me very much, but what had the most impact on me during the conference was a short talk by a young man. With a joyful heart and a broad grin he shared an idea for reaching the Muslim world with the claims of the Lord Jesus Christ.

Frankly, his idea sounded crazy. He and some colleagues planned to send people with tape recorders into Muslim countries. These people would then walk through cities, towns and villages, and record the names of streets and people on the tapes. The names and addresses they selected in that way would later be transcribed from the tapes and sent to Christians in Europe and America. These Christians would then send specially printed letters directly to these Muslims to share the good news about Jesus Christ with them.

Yes, a crazy plan. With that same broad grin, the young man added that they had no money for the project, they had hardly any staff, they wanted to work in countries completely closed to the Gospel, and their goal was to reach millions for the Lord Jesus Christ.

But crazy as it was, this dream, this vision impressed me very much. It showed me that this young man and the people he worked with had a real vision. It showed their willingness to be obedient to the Lord's command to go and make disciples of all nations. But above all, this impossible plan revealed to me their great love for the Lord.

After the meeting, I went back to my room. I felt ashamed. I thought of the Netherlands, of the thousands of Christians, of the media available there, of the wealth of the country. I felt ashamed because I suddenly realised that in spite of all that had happened, we were still not doing all we could to reach our country with the Gospel. We had still not reached everyone in the country with our news of abundant spiritual food.

Alone in my room, I began to ask myself some new questions. 'Where is our vision? Where is our love for the Lord Jesus Christ? Why are we not more obedient? Don't we have the courage to step out in faith to believe that the impossible could happen?'

I wrestled with these questions for several days. For two nights I didn't sleep a wink. During this restless but very precious and holy time, God gave me the desire and the vision for a nation-wide evangelistic outreach in the Netherlands. Even though at that time I had only a vague idea of how to do it, I was convinced that it had to be one great united effort to bring the Gospel into every home in the country.

During one of those nights when I was wide awake, I saw very clearly the spiritual need of my country. I thought of the fact that so many people were living in despair. Millions were afraid of a nuclear war. Countless homes were broken. People were lonely. Men and women were hurting deep inside because they had no answers to the basic questions in life. That night God gave me the theme for the nationwide outreach: There is Hope.

Planning for the impossible

After the conference I went home and nervously shared the vision with some of our staff and a few of the country's Christian leaders. I must admit that not all of them shared my enthusiasm, but that didn't stop me! So, along with two capable and loyal members of my staff, I started planning this nationwide outreach. We met in the home of one of my colleagues and − much to his wife's dismay − the whole living room was soon plastered with diagrams, schedules and budgets. We had a great time planning something so vast that our minds could not take it in.

A few months later, after hours of prayer, planning and talking to various people, we were ready to launch our plan on an unsuspecting Christian community. At a national meeting of the

Evangelical Alliance we were allowed to share our vision and our plans. They were gracious enough to give us a platform for our impossible dream, and that was to become an important step in the long route towards a national campaign. Even though the response at that first meeting was mixed, at least the Christian leaders knew what was going to happen.

Our next step was to hire a large meeting hall in the centre of the country. We called for a national day of repentance and prayer. More than 3,500 Christians from all over the country attended that unique prayer gathering, and we introduced the plans for a nationwide evangelistic outreach. At last the news was out. The press picked up the story. Soon most of the evangelical Christians in the country knew that 'There is Hope' was coming.

But more important than any of that, Christians began to pray. Prayer seminars were held in many parts of the country. Prayer groups were formed. The foundation was laid.

There was still much to be done, however. Christians had to learn how to share their faith in a personal, natural way with relatives, friends and neighbours. Hundreds of church training seminars were held throughout the country. The demand for this training was so high that our resources were completely overwhelmed. Other Christian organisations, like the Navigators, stepped in to help. Where it still proved impossible to do the training ourselves we sent a video of the training course out to the churches. It was not the ideal way to train Christians, but at the time it was the only way we could meet the huge demand.

By the end of February 1982, after many months of hard work by pastors, church members, project leaders and the staff of several organizations, Christians in the Netherlands were ready for the largest evangelistic outreach our country had known.

All over Europe

Before I get into this 'Hope-Campaign' in more detail, it is good to know that this evangelistic outreach was not the first in Europe and was in no way unique. In Finland a nationwide evangelistic campaign started in the spring of 1979. Markku Happonen, a Finnish Lutheran pastor, who served as the director of the movement comments:

> Altogether, I consider it a high privilege to have been involved in something like this in Finland. The challenges that we faced in fulfilling the vision God had called us to, were way beyond our capacities, resources and capabilities. But when, after strong hesitation and inner struggles, I finally said, "Yes, Lord, I am available! Please lead me!", I then found myself in the midst of the most exciting process of my life thus far: being totally dependent upon God in things I had never tried before. God led us step by step, answered prayers, and did miracles in and through human lives. Sharing the joy with others who had the same experience was incomparable. Dozens of pastors experienced fulfilment in their lives as a result of their motivation, and sensed the meaningfulness of what they were doing. I shared their struggles and even their despair at certain moments when difficulties seemed to be overwhelming, and rejoiced in God's solutions to the problems. There were rays of new identity of being a Christian and a new sense of being an active church member shining into the lives of thousands of so-called average, nominal Christians.

Personal relationships with Christ became new, life-changing realities. Humbly and gratefully, I look back, thinking and remembering all of this; I pray that this vision will spread to every country in Europe, and the churches can benefit from these kinds of efforts, resulting in renewal and revival.

Similar evangelistic campaigns have been held in Northern Ireland, Portugal, Scotland, Switzerland and Spain. José Monells, a Baptist pastor from Barcelona, recalls:

It is a joy to see how God honours the faith of Christians who are serious about the Great Commission and how God often does much more than we can ever dream of. When the vision grew in our hearts to develop city-wide evangelistic campaigns in our nice, warm, Catholic country, we decided to start at the top. So we wrote to the King of Spain and requested an audience with him to explain our dreams. Much to our amazement, His Majesty King Juan Carlos I invited us to the palace and we had a chance to share with him the purpose of the campaign and, more importantly, the love of Christ.

So, the first thing our vision did was to open doors for the Gospel in the highest places of our country. Later we also organized a special dinner attended by about 150 distinguished political, cultural and media leaders, and a breakfast meeting for another 500 church leaders and businessmen. During all these meetings we shared our objectives and the philosophy of the movement we wanted to see develop in our country.

Many more exciting stories like this could be told, of new visions and of Christians who stepped out in faith to do the seemingly impossible. Stories of God's blessings and changed lives. Stories of mini-revivals in Christian groups and in churches. It happened and is still happening all over Europe. In many countries Christians are dreaming and planning to proclaim the message of hope in Christ to their city or to the whole nation. Some day all these different evangelistic activities are going to flow together into one mighty river of Christian testimony all over Europe. A fresh and living river that will touch millions of people. A powerful stream of God's grace that will be a blessing to many nations.

Chapter 4

The heart of hope

Let's get down to basics: what exactly is a 'There is Hope' campaign? What is involved if a church or group decides to participate in a local or even national evangelistic outreach? How is a project organized? What about preparation for church members? How are people who show an interest drawn into a church and effectively discipled?

In a nutshell, a 'There is Hope' campaign is an opportunity for churches and Christian groups to pray together for revival and to work together in evangelism, with the aim of exposing the whole population of an area to the Gospel of the Lord Jesus Christ. It is a strategy for encouraging the maximum co-operation between churches, yet giving them complete freedom in how they use the project. The 'There is Hope' strategy can also work very effectively in universities, holiday camps . . . and in YOUR neighbourhood.

Besides vision, that really is the starting motor of any campaign, and the content of the message which is dealt with in a later chapter, there are seven building blocks at the heart of 'There is Hope'. These building blocks provide a basis and a skeleton for the campaign. They are crucial for an effective campaign but they are not enough in themselves. Flesh and blood need to be added to the skeleton before it will come to life.

So 'There is Hope' is not a ready-made, off-the-shelf package that you can apply to your own situation. It is a basic strategy with the potential to be tailor-made by each church and group to fit its own situation.

For this reason, 'There is Hope' campaigns can all end up being somewhat different, although they are based on the same building blocks. The overall goal is to reach as many people as possible over and over again with the message of hope in Jesus. To reach that goal, the campaign has to be done in a way that is relevant to both recipients and the senders of the message. It is important, for example, that every 'There is Hope' campaign reflects the colour and creativity of its message. It's a familiar but true saying that the medium is the message. In other words, you cannot package a message of life and expect people to believe it if the whole thing looks drab and the messenger looks sober and sad. When those four lepers returned to the city, their message was bursting with life and excitement. Ours should do the same!

In this chapter I would like to share with you the seven building blocks of a 'There is Hope' campaign. It does not really matter whether we have a nation-wide, city-wide, a church campaign or even a neighbourhood campaign in mind. The seven building blocks are valid for any size campaign.

Also, it is good to realize that this book is not a training manual but rather an idea-source and a vision-builder. Much more can and has to be said if you want to be used by God to set up an evangelistic campaign. Special vision conferences are organized regularly and more information is available for those who want to step out in faith and do the impossible.

Building block no. 1

The use of the media to get through to all people

One of the unique features of a 'There is Hope' campaign is that its goal is to reach the entire population of an area, city or country. The aim is to bring the right spiritual food to every single resident — families, housewives, businessmen, students, the elderly, children, the unemployed.

One of the best ways to do this is through the use of the media. We live in an age of mass communication: television, radio, newspapers, magazines, books, advertisements, direct mail — the list is endless. We Christians should make the most of the media to proclaim the message of hope. It is important not only because it will help people to come closer to God or to accept the Lord Jesus Christ as their Saviour, but a media campaign can also change the atmosphere in a city or a country. It can create an environment in which it becomes easier for Christians to share their faith. Jesus can become the topic of conversation in the community.

☆　☆　☆

I will never forget the day the campaign started. All around the city you could see posters and billboards proclaiming the love of our Lord Jesus Christ. Special pamphlets were sent out through the post and many people heard the Christian message either via the telephone or during a personal visit by a church member.

One woman I know of personally was at the point of committing suicide when she saw one of the advertisements and contacted the campaign centre. There she invited Jesus Christ into her life and she is now a member of one of the churches in Barcelona. Jesus gave her spiritual life and also saved her physical life (José Monells, director of 'Vida para', Spain)

☆ ☆ ☆

During the last week of January 1981 when the campaign started, I was driving in Helsinki with my closest co-worker, Pastor Pekka Paakkanen. We could not believe what we saw. The whole city was covered with our campaign media. It was impossible to be out on the street and not see it. The same was true in all other cities as well

Through combined media, the church and its message became a public issue. In the cities where the campaigns were held, over 89 per cent of the population knew the slogans and had heard that the church was involved in a massive outreach. Even at other locations, one-third of the people were aware of these activities. When people arrived at work, colleagues would ask each other, 'Did they already call you from the church?'

The media campaigns brought the message through to such an extent that, in March of 1982, the campaign slogan was granted the award of the best-noticed poster in Finland during 1981.

In addition to the advertising of the churches on billboards, lamp-post posters, windows of shops, various stickers, buttons, plastic bags and milk cartons, there was a very high interest in the campaign on the part of the secular media and the press.

This publicity was helpful and was needed to prepare the contacts that took place during the outreach. The major approach was to call every home in the area. Where there were fewer telephones, home visits were made as well.

Also, a church newspaper and a campaign booklet with personal testimonies and a clear Gospel presentation were distributed to each home. This way practically all the two million people at these locations were reached, two-thirds of them through personal contact.

Every evening, during an almost two-week long period, about 50,000 telephone calls were made by the campaign workers. Nine out of ten who were called wanted to talk with a representative of the church. Two-thirds of the people thought that this kind of approach was positive, where only one-tenth felt negatively about it. Over half (65 per cent) of all phone calls included discussions about faith on a personal level, thus one-fourth of the conversations were recorded as relatively long. It is obvious that thousands of people found new life in Jesus Christ — or started the process to find out more about Him.'
(Markku Happonen, director of 'Tassa Elama', Finland.)

☆   ☆   ☆

In the Netherlands we produced a magazine which was delivered free to every single home in the country. The cover showed a large colourful rainbow with the slogan 'There is Hope'.

Its forty-eight pages were full of news about the hope that Jesus Christ has to offer.

Through articles about despair that can turn into hope, the uniqueness of the Bible and testimonies by well-known Christians, the gospel was shared. Colourful, easy-to-digest spiritual food.

47

The magazine was distributed to every household in the Netherlands. More than five million copies of this messenger of hope found their way into Dutch homes. Its message of good news went out to a whole nation.

Nothing like this had ever happened before in the history of the Netherlands. A survey showed that by the spring of 1982, 78 per cent of the Dutch population had, in one way or another, been in touch with the 'There is Hope' campaign. Yes, at long last we were sharing the good news of abundant food with the whole nation. Like the four lepers, we had finally gone back to our 'city' to proclaim a message of hope and deliverance.

Building block no. 2

Personal evangelism

The distribution of a magazine and a live television programme marked the beginning of the nationwide 'There is Hope' campaign in the Netherlands. These were probably the most visible aspects of the outreach, but they were by no means the most significant.

Far more important were the local evangelistic activities that came hot on the heels of the magazine distribution and television programme. Hundreds of churches in more than 250 cities, towns and villages started their own evangelistic 'There is Hope' projects at the same time. The gospel of hope was shared in a wide variety of ways, all of them personal, with hundreds of thousands of people. Christians went from door to door to talk about Jesus. Telephones were used to find the people who were most interested in the Gospel. Ladies and couples held evangelistic meetings in their own homes. Large events for children were staged. There were special church services, film evenings, evangelistic concerts, open-air meetings; you name it, we tried it.

The media campaigns and events really acted as a kind of strainer to find the people who were most interested in the Gospel. All the publicity served to 'load' as many people as possible into the top of the strainer. However, only a certain percentage of people responded to the message of hope, and fell, so to speak, through the strainer. The Christians then concentrated on those people.

Building block no. 3

Training of Christians

Picture a huge football stadium, crowded with thousands of fans watching two teams running round doing all the work. It's basically the same in the church. But 'There is Hope' is all about taking the 22 exhausted players off the field and using them to coach the thousands of eager fans.

'There is Hope' is a movement for ordinary Christians – a revolution of laity. Church members are the evangelists rather than big-name speakers (although these can still form an integral part of a campaign). The campaign is merely set up to create an environment which makes its easier for Christians to share their faith. Church members should be kept informed and involved right from the conception of the campaign. The 'success' of a church's participation will be directly linked to this. It is essential that ordinary Christians are given practical help, especially in three areas: prayer, personal evangelism and leading Bible study groups.

Prayer is the real foundation for a campaign.

Even though most Christians would agree with that, it is also true that most Christians struggle with their personal prayer time. The first and the most important thing we can do for a campaign is to raise up an army of prayer warriors — a group of Christians who are both motivated and trained to continually lift the whole outreach before the Lord.

Personal evangelism is the focal point of a 'There is Hope' campaign. All activities should be aimed at bringing Christians and non-Christians together. When that happens the Christian needs to know how to share his faith, to know what to say and when to be silent. It is only through theoretical and practical training that a Christian will learn and feel free to talk openly about Jesus.

Leading Bible study groups is the main vehicle for follow-up. Over and over again we have learned that the best environment for a person to grow in his faith is in a small group. One-to-one follow-up is fine too, but it sometimes becomes a threat to the new Christian. Follow-up through church services is impersonal and will most often not meet the needs of the young Christian. However, proper follow-up in small church Bible study groups will often lead to church involvement later on.

If all this kind of training is not available within the church itself, the resources can and should be found elsewhere. Proper preparation will encourage both the spiritual growth of church members and the effectiveness of the church in communicating Jesus Christ to its neighbourhood.

Sometimes we have to be creative in providing the training for church members. In the Netherlands hundreds of church training seminars were simultaneously held throughout the country.

immediately before the campaign started, the demand for this training was so high that our resources were totally overwhelmed. Other Christian organizations stepped in to help, but it was still impossible to meet the needs. So we spent three days in a video studio, and put the whole training on video. Churches who asked for training at the last moment received several video tapes. This was certainly not the ideal way to train Christians, but at that time it was the only way we could meet the huge demand.

Building block no. 4

Home Bible Fellowship

Setting up a city-wide or nationwide evangelistic campaign is not easy, but even more difficult is providing ongoing quality follow-up for people who have been touched by the campaign in one way or another.

The 'spiritual success' of a campaign is to a large extent determined by the care we show for those who want to know more about Jesus, those who have committed their lives to Him, and Christians who want to grow in their faith. Therefore anyone contacted during the course of a campaign who shows an interest should be invited to a Home Bible Fellowship. A small, informal group like this will provide a vital link in that person's growth in understanding of spiritual matters. The ideal leader would be a responsible, mature Christian who can create an environment conducive to good discussion.

☆　☆　☆

Ten years ago Home Bible Fellowships were an exception in Swiss State churches. Now the majority of churches have one or more Bible groups meeting in homes where Christians read the Bible, discuss its application and enjoy fellowship with one another. These Bible groups are increasingly becoming the spring-board for many social and missionary activities as they try to reach their neighbourhood with the love of Jesus Christ. There are as many op-portunities to show God's love in a practical way in a country where the majority of in-habitants do not know why they live, and where many people suffer from isolation and have few friendly and fulfilling relationships. As a result of 'Aktion Neues Leben' in Switzer-land, 3,700 Bible study groups came into ex-istence. In these informal groups participants start by reading and studying the Gospel of John'.

(Hanspeter Nüesch, director 'Aktion Neues Leben', Switzerland.)

In Finland, 3,000 new, small groups were estab-lished with 23,000 participants after our nation-wide evangelistic campaign, and this was only the beginning. According to the Research Institute of the Church of Finland, in a recent report covering four years, by the end of 1983 the number of small groups in city congregations in Finland had inc-reased 75.5 per cent compared to the situation before the campaigns (1979).

Together with these 'newcomers', the cam-paign volunteers are a tremendous new resource for local congregations in their future activities. Hundreds of church workers and thousands of lay people received new en-couragement and experience in bringing the Gospel to their fellow citizens.'

(Markku Happonen, director of 'Tassa Elama', Finland.)

Building block no. 5

Local church activities

The essence of a 'There is Hope' campaign is that the 'lepers' share the good news with the people they know are in need. In a 'Hope' project, therefore, it is the local church which is the primary agency for evangelism. Christian organizations and well-known evangelists may help and encourage, but the bulk of the work has to be done by the local Christians. Each church involved in a 'There is Hope' project sets up its own committee with the task of stimulating prayer, making sure church members are properly trained, coming up with creative ideas to apply 'There is Hope' to their particular community, and ensuring that the necessary finances are found.

To give you an idea of the role that a local church can play in a 'There is Hope' campaign, I have asked Myles Wilson, a former director of 'Project Hope' in Northern Ireland, to share what happened during the region-wide outreach in one of the most politically unstable areas of Western Europe.

☆ ☆ ☆

Northern Ireland has, for centuries, been divided into two main cultures based on religious differences. This drastically affects the life of the body of Christ. In general, churches operate in isolation, as if under seige. An underlying feeling that they need to defend themselves against the traditions of other churches severely limits any real co-operation in church life and outreach.

Our task was two-fold. We wanted to help bring the message of hope in Christ to every family in Ulster in a way that would be understood, and we wanted to encourage believers to use the opportunities created by such a project to present the Gospel to those around them. The plan was to deliver a high-quality, colour magazine to every home throughout the country during Easter week of 1986. This would continue as churches of every denomination highlighted the Hope theme throughout the spring and summer to encourage their own congregations and to promote evangelism. The 'Jesus' film, a motion picture about the life of Christ based on the Gospel of St Luke, would also be shown in cinemas, and as much publicity as possible would be used to create an atmosphere in which it was easier to talk about hope in Christ. Schools throughout the country would receive educational packages for use in religious education classes, focusing on the 'There is Hope' theme.

The Hope theme was adopted by more than 300 churches and the more creative they were, the more fruitful the results. Men's breakfasts, women's coffee mornings, special rainbow events for children, family meals, visits to old people's homes to talk about hope, and door-to-door work, all raised the profile of the Gospel.

A member of one of the fellowships which used the Hope theme right through to the summer told me: 'The Hope project is continuing to be a real blessing. It's provided a ready-made avenue for us to go into people's homes and to pray and share Jesus. It has stimulated our ongoing evangelism – thank you!'

In Lurgan, near where we live, one church had their Hope campaign in October. Twenty people accepted Christ.

In our own church a special Hope children's

week was held with more than 100 children coming each night. Fifteen of them asked for counselling and my wife Phyllis had the privilege of leading one of these to the Lord.

Two thousand magazines were sent into prisons and we know for sure that one prisoner became a Christian as a result. He is now in contact with the Prison Fellowship.

The 'Jesus' film showings were a high point of the project. A total of 13,000 people saw the film. In Belfast the cinema manager moved to a bigger screen and retained it for a third week. He remarked that 'even without publicity, "Jesus" is bringing in larger crowds than "Out of Africa".' If we had realized how successful the film was to be, we would have encouraged other cinema owners to show it and would have done more to promote the accompanying Bible study and special edition of St Luke's Gospel.

History was made as a result of 'There is Hope' when the Catholic Bishop of Down and Connor, Dr. Daly, and the then moderator of the Presbyterian Church, Dr. Dickinson, spoke together on the theme in one of the province's largest Presbyterian churches. This was the first time in 400 years that such an event had taken place. The occasion highlighted the possibility of greater understanding between churches, but the presence of loud protesters, who had to be removed by police, re-emphasized how deeply the suspicion and bitterness run. Many of these protesters professed personal faith in Christ.

Tragedy has often been the powerful setting for seeing God's Spirit at work. We saw this in vivid detail during the campaign. A Christian brother, a policeman and father of five children, was enthusiastically promoting the Hope outreach in his area. He was shot dead — for being a policeman. His brother, a minister, and his congregation responded by being all the more zealous to present hope in Christ to their community.

There is hope for Northern Ireland! Of that I'm now convinced. Christians emerged during Project Hope who are willing to walk the necessary tightrope in order to present Christ. In Holywood, just outside Belfast, five different churches — four Protestant and one Catholic — joined ranks to publicize Hope functions in each of their churches: a rare occurrence.

☆　☆　☆

Building block no. 6

Working together

I once saw a series of dramatic pictures in a magazine that I will never forget. The first picture showed an aerial view of an enormous yellow wheat-field. In the middle of the field was a little dark spot; the farmhouse.

The second picture showed a close-up of the farmer, his wife and a few children frantically searching for their three-year-old son and brother who had wandered into the wheat-field. In the third picture you could see a large group of people searching together for the little boy. The fourth picture was dark and gloomy. It was after sunset. The people had joined hands and walked like a human chain through the enormous wheat-field. They had started to systematically search for the boy. The last picture brought tears to my eyes. It showed the father, holding his dead three-year-old son. He cried out: 'My God, if we had started to hold hands earlier, my son might live.'

There are millions of 'dying' sons and daughters all over Europe. One of the reasons for this is that we Christians have never really learned to join hands in searching for the lost. We may be active and work hard, but we have never learned to work together in proclaiming the hopeful message of the Gospel. I am sure that God cries like the father of that little boy: 'Oh, if they were only willing to join hands and work together to search for the lost people of Western Europe.'

Now, I know that there are many barriers to working together as churches and Christian organizations, but an experience I've often had is that a plan for a united evangelistic outreach can draw Christians together in a new way.

Distributing identical literature and arranging coinciding activities under the common theme of 'There is Hope' can be a powerful demonstration of unity in Christ. Literature should emphasize truths that are central to most churches. But efforts to establish detailed agreement on theology or practice should be avoided or the campaign will never get off the ground! Each church involved should agree to respect the sincerely held beliefs of the others. The basis of our hope, summarized in the apostle Paul's words, is: '. . . that Christ died for our sins according to the Scriptures, that He was buried, that He was raised on the third day according to the Scriptures . . .' (I Corinthians 15:3,4)

This common hope should be enough to draw us together in love and concern for the starving. Spirit-produced unity across the denominational divide will make our witness all the more powerful. Remember too that the Lord 'commands' blessings where His people are living in unity. (Psalm 133)

To make sure that the maximum co-operation between churches is achieved, a local committee of mature men and women should also be set up to co-ordinate the work of the different church committees. This team shoulders the overall responsibility for the project. Their practical tasks include legal accountability, choosing campaign literature, making the most of the 'There is Hope' logo, raising and handling the necessary finances, and co-ordinating the different churches' plans.

☆   ☆   ☆

Christians from the most different church traditions worked hand in hand. Protestants with Catholics, Baptists with Methodists, Pentecostals with members of the Salvation Army. The Lord Jesus Christ and the experience of a Spirit-given new life united the Christians. They realized that the enormous task of calling back the Swiss population to God and obedience to His Word could only be accomplished by putting all their strength together.

Within eight years 780 churches of all denominations have reached out to their neighbourhoods. Over 25,000 volunteer workers have contacted by phone and personal visits more than a million households. They offered a free evangelistic booklet called 'Neues Leben' or in Swiss German 'Nois Läbe' and invited the interested people to a Bible discussion group. More than 770,000 people requested the booklet.'

(Hanspeter Nüesch, director 'Aktion Neues Leben', Switzerland.)

Building block no. 7

Prayer — the real foundation

The Old Testament leader Nehemiah prayed, wept and fasted for four months for the city he loved. The rebuilding of the walls of Jerusalem was a direct result of the repentance and constant prayers of this one man. Moses, Ezra, Daniel, Jeremiah and many others all prayed and fasted for their people and their country. In the same way anything we do for our people and our country has to be based on a firm foundation of prayer.

The Swiss 'Aktion Neues Leben' (Action New Life), that touched the major part of Switzerland in a few years, started with seven 24-hour prayer chains. In six years 750 prayer seminars of three evenings each were held all over the country resulting in many prayer groups and other activities. In Finland, the churches held a national prayer weekend attended by about 8,000 people. In Edinburgh, Scotland, a small group of Christians started meeting every month to pray for their campaign. Thirty people attended the first meeting; that number went up to 60 and then to 120. The week before the campaign started 2,300 Christians met together to pray for their city. Here is an account by David Hill, the chairman of 'There is Hope', Edinburgh, about the special ways God responded to the prayers of His children.

☆　☆　☆

It was an exciting day for all of us. We had seen it as a step of faith ten months previously to book the Usher Hall in the centre of Edinburgh for a prayer meeting. This was to be the launch of 'There is Hope'. Some would have thought it foolish — I think we would have too, except that we sensed God was in it. The 2,500 seats seemed a lot to fill, and in our weaker moments we joked about seeing if we could bulk-purchase some shop models to fill the empty seats. Having booked it the previous June, we inevitably got lost in all the activities of planning 'There is Hope': contacting churches, planning meetings, developing training, prayer meetings, and so on.

There were two significant milestones we had to pass. The first was the church involvement. Our initial goal of '20 to 30 churches' gradually became 'up to 30 churches', and finally '30 churches' exactly. The Lord must have smiled on us the morning we had to send the names of the churches involved to the printers. We had only 29! What about number 30? I decided to make one last phone call to a church which had been on the brink of getting involved. 'Yes, I'm very sorry we haven't been back to you,' came the reply. 'and we would like to be involved'.

The other milestone was the bus advertising. The sight of 70 buses driving around Edinburgh bearing a bright rainbow and the 'There is Hope' slogan was a marvellous sight. It also provoked some curiosity, and provided an opportunity to answer people's questions with the news that 'There is hope because Jesus is alive.' But for the Christians, the buses were special. Having been told at the last minute that we would not be able to advertise on the buses, having prayed, and then having seen a council meeting unanimously overturn an earlier decision against us, we felt God had intervened. God was giving victory to His people. Interestingly, we heard some time later that one of the advertising agency employees whose joy it was to paste the adverts on the buses has become a Christian!

It was lovely to see a few real rainbows in the sky around Eastertime, too. The best one was on the afternoon of Good Friday – a brilliant double rainbow which, as we looked at it from our back window, made a huge arch over Edinburgh Castle. This was advertising we hadn't paid for and perhaps the Lord's way of telling us that there is hope for Edinburgh.

So Easter Saturday 1986 arrived and 2,300 people came to the Usher Hall to pray for revival. It was a powerful meeting. Many had never been in a meeting like this before. I had not. There was a lot of singing. A choir of 250 people helped lead the praise, backed by a band of competent musicians. God gave me a message about gathering together: 'O Edinburgh, how I long to gather you as a hen gathers her chicks under her wings.' Then we broke into groups of three or four people to pray for our city.

The murmuring of quiet prayer was heard around the whole building. The Lord was there. Some people were uncomfortable for a while. One or two cried. Someone who was not a Christian gave his heart to the Lord. A young man from Militant Tendency had wandered in to see what was happening, and found himself in a prayer group with a Pentecostal gentleman and a Brethren lady. He was somewhat overawed. Many people prayed out loud for the first time in their lives. Hundreds sensed the Lord's presence and were blessed. What a meeting!

✫   ✫   ✫

Now, of course, there are many different ways in which we can pray: large prayer meetings, prayer conferences, prayer groups, prayer telephones, personal prayer and so on. It does not really matter what form of prayer we choose, as long as the whole campaign is bathed in prayer.

Prayer is the key. It has to be the spiritual foundation for any work we do for the Kingdom of God. 'Unless the Lord builds the house, its builders labour in vain". (Psalm 127:1)

Putting it all together

So we see that the seven building blocks — media, personal evangelism, training, Home Bible Fellowships, the local church, co-operation and prayer — together with vision and the right message make a 'There is Hope' campaign.

As mentioned earlier all these ingredients have to be part of a campaign. Leave one out and the evangelistic outreach will be less successful.

At the same time all these building blocks should be related to the possibilities and the needs of the local situation. This means that a lot of creativity is needed to organize a campaign in such a way that it reaches the secularized people but at the same time enhances the support and involvement of local churches and individual Christians.

Once God has given the vision for a campaign, a lot of prayer, wisdom and creativity is needed to turn the vision into an exciting reality.

But what about this last building block, the message of hope that we want to proclaim?

Chapter 5

A message of hope

When we published the first evangelistic magazine in the Netherlands, which went to each of the five million homes in the country, we made a mistake. The mistake was that in the magazine we showed the hope that Jesus Christ has to offer against the despair in human life and in this world. But no one is interested to read about the despair he already experiences. People want to know the answer. They want to hear a positive message. A message about hope, love, joy, peace and a happy future. And that is what the message of Jesus Christ is all about.

Therefore, when the movement in the Netherlands continued and when we published more magazines, we left all the despair out. We only communicated the hope that Jesus Christ has to offer.

Now, what exactly is this hope? What is the message of hope that we Christians, ambassadors of the Lord Jesus Christ here on earth, can share? What exactly do we 'lepers' tell the desperate and starving people in the 'city' of Europe?

Basically this living hope has three different threads which are closely entwined with one another. First there is the personal hope that Jesus Christ offers to each individual. Closely related to that is the hope that He offers to our society at large, and both the personal hope for the individual and the hope for society culminate in the hope that Jesus Christ offers for an eternal future.

Hope for the individual

When I met the Lord Jesus Christ as my personal Saviour I was on the verge of committing suicide. I was only 20, but fed up with life. My basic problem was that I had not been able to find satisfactory answers to what I considered to be basic questions in life: 'Who am I? Where do I come from? Where am I going?'

Because I had been unable to find the answers to those questions within myself, and because no one else seemed to have any answers either, I began to experiment with life. The only result, however, was that my problems multiplied and any hope I had had of finding real answers almost completely vanished. It was like desperately trying to climb out of a dark and slippery pit, but all the time sliding further and further down. The more I experienced, and the harder I tried to find answers, the deeper I slipped into this pit. And I knew that at the bottom of the pit there was only a dark, meaningless death.

Then, in the midst of all this, a man started to talk to me about Jesus. He talked about his love for the Lord Jesus Christ and the purpose in life that this relationship gave him. He spoke with great joy. I did not like hearing it and I simply could not believe it was true, but since the man happened to be my boss in the art studio where I was working, I pretended to be interested!

These dishonest discussions went on for several months: he went on sharing, I went on politely pretending to be interested. But even though I was not interested in what he said, somehow his message started to get through to me. I decided to buy a Bible and check for myself. For the first time in my life I started to read the Gospel of Matthew and I must admit that its message grabbed me immediately. I discovered that Matthew was writing about someone who knew what He was living for; someone who had a clear goal and purpose in life: the Lord Jesus Christ. Then I came to a verse that turned my life upside down. 'Come to me, all you who are weary and burdened, and I will give you rest.'(Matthew 11:28)

That really hit me between the eyes. This was exactly what I had been looking for so desperately; rest, inner peace and meaning in life. Here someone was offering to give me exactly what I had longed for. It was too good to be true — and consequently I had a hard time believing it! I wrestled with it for several months. Sometimes I could believe this was the most beautiful truth there was. The next day I'd be back to believing it was a dirty lie.

This continued until I came to the point of realizing I couldn't go on like this. I remember being very clearly aware that I had only two options left in life. One was to opt out of life altogether and finish it. The other was to follow Jesus. In utter despair and hopelessness I finally fell on my knees one evening and dedicated my life to God. My prayer was simple: 'Lord, there are many things about You I don't understand, but I want to come to You; please give me rest.'

That was in January 1968. As look back I know that that simple prayer marked the beginning of a dramatic change in my life. Something very real happened within me that day; The light was suddenly switched on; I found myself on solid ground and with a bright future ahead of me.

Why am I telling you all this?

First of all to emphasize the hope that Jesus Christ offers to an individual.

Any individual.

Of course my testimony is by no means unique. There are millions of stories just like mine. Jesus Christ has given new life to the most desperate people. He has healed broken relationships and He has given hope to people in the most hopeless situations.

The second reason I shared my own story is to honour the man who had the courage to talk to me about Jesus. He was a good and faithful ambassador for the Lord. If it hadn't been for him and the message of hope he passed on to me, I probably wouldn't be around any more.

But, let's face it, talking about Jesus is not always easy. In fact it can be very difficult to share your faith. Even though I am committed to being a witness of the Lord Jesus it is sometimes not easy for me to go to people and share my faith. And because of this built-in apprehension that seems to be part of life, I was very happy when someone many years ago taught me a simple and direct way to share my faith. He showed me a little booklet called 'Knowing God Personally' (details of which are given at the end of the book). He then explained to me how I could use this simple tool to explain the way of salvation and to encourage people to accept the Lord Jesus Christ as their personal Saviour.

I would also like to encourage you to use the booklet to share your faith. When you get an opportunity to talk to someone about Christ, you can simply introduce the booklet and read through it together. Take time to explain or illustrate the four points that are made in the booklet. Don't be afraid to ask the other person about his or her opinion of the booklet, or to ask where he or she stands in relationship to Jesus. And, if the person is ready to receive Jesus Christ in his heart as personal Saviour and Lord, you can lead him through the prayer of commitment outlined in the booklet.

I realize that all this may sound over-simplified and too good to be true, but without exaggerating I can assure you that millions of people all over the world have come into a personal relationship with the Lord Jesus Christ through the use of this little booklet.

I have used this simple but powerful presentation of the Gospel over and over again. Often I have found myself talking to a person that was prepared by the Holy Spirit to follow the Lord Jesus. Many times I have had the privilege of leading a person in a prayer of commitment to Jesus. And always it has been a great joy to be used by God to draw people to Himself.

Therefore, if you have never led another person to Jesus Christ, or if you are not sharing your faith regularly, I would strongly like to encourage you to start doing so. As a Christian you need to share your faith to stay close to the Lord and to grow in Him. The non-Christian needs you sharing your faith in order to meet Him who gives new life and real hope for the future.

Let me encourage you to ask the Lord to show you with whom you could share your faith. Go to that person and use the 'Knowing God Personally' booklet to talk about Jesus. And if the person is open to accept the Lord Jesus Christ as his personal Saviour, don't hesitate to lead him in a prayer of commitment. And if that person is not ready to follow Jesus, rejoice anyway. God is in control. The Holy Spirit will do His work. Effective witnessing is simply talking about Jesus in the power of the Holy Spirit and leaving the results to God.

Hope for the country

In II Chronicles 7:14 we read the following words spoken by the Lord God to King Solomon in a dream: '. . . if My people, who are called by My name, will humble themselves and pray and seek My face and turn from their wicked ways, then will I hear from heaven and will forgive their sin and will heal their land.'

These words were directed at the people of Israel at a particular time in their history. But, like so many truths in the Bible, these ancient words also have a clear message for us today. If we, the people of God, humble ourselves, pray, seek the Lord and turn from our sins, then God will also forgive us and restore our lands. The greater number of dedicated Christians there are in a country, the greater the impact on that land through their way of life and through their proclamation of the Gospel. God will work *through* dedicated Christians to touch the rest of a society. But, even more importantly, God Himself will work directly in a society *because* of the presence of His children. He will answer their prayers and He Himself will bring about things beyond anything Christians could ever have dreamed of. He will heal the land.

'Through the blessing of the upright a city is exalted.' (Proverbs 11:11a) This is a Biblical promise and I will illustrate its truth with three examples: a story from the Old Testament, one from the New Testament, and an event which took place in Europe this century.

At the time of King Josiah (about 630 BC), Judah, the southern part of the divided kingdom of Israel, had fallen into all kinds of sin. The nation was in spiritual and moral darkness. People worshipped Baal, the sun, the moon and the stars. All over the country there were altars, statues and shrines to heathen gods — on the hill-tops, in the valleys and on the roof of the king's palace. There were statues of horses and chariots near the temple entrance. There was even a statue of a grotesque idol inside God's temple itself. Outside the same temple male prostitutes sold their bodies as a sacrifice to idols. During special festivities parents forced their children to walk through fire until they were dead, as a sacrifice to Molech.

Israel had become a wicked nation, filthy in God's sight. Yet within a very short space of time the situation was to change completely. God sent a dramatic revival that was started by the young King Josiah. This spiritual awakening had a fan-tastic impact on society. Almost the whole of 2 Kings 23 is devoted to the moral and social changes brought about by this revival. We read how they destroyed all the equipment used to worship Baal. The idol was taken from the temple and burned. The male prostitutes' homes were torn down and the altars, shrines and statues were destroyed. Everything that stood against the Lord was removed from the country. Every dim-ension of society was affected by what happened.

In Acts 19 we can see another occasion when the word of God had a huge impact on society. In verses 17 and 18 we read that the name of Jesus was held in high honour in the city of Ephesus and that many of the new believers publicly con-fessed their evil deeds. Some who had practised sorcery brought their scrolls together and burned them. When they later calculated the value of the scrolls they discovered that their total value was

50,000 drachmas — that's about 1.5 million pounds sterling in today's money. The revival in Ephesus affected society so much that a riot broke out. Businessmen who had sold silver shrines and were losing trade started the uproar and soon the whole city was involved.

In his book 'Evangelical Awakenings 1900', the Belfast-born Dr. J. Edwin Orr records many examples of the powerful effect that the Gospel can have on society. He writes:

☆　☆　☆

The story of the Welsh revival (at the beginning of this century) is astounding. Begun with prayer meetings of less than a score of intercessors, when it burst its bounds the churches of Wales were crowded for more than two years. A hundred thousand outsiders were converted and added to the churches, the vast majority remaining true to the end. Drunkenness was immediately cut in half, and many taverns went bankrupt. Crime was so diminished that judges were presented with white gloves signifying that there were no cases of murder, assault, rape, robbery or the like to consider. The police became "unemployed" in many districts. Stoppages occurred in coal mines, not due to unpleasantness between management and workers, but because so many foul-mouthed miners became converted and stopped using foul language that the horses which hauled the coal trucks in the mines could no longer understand what was being said to them, and the transportation ground to a halt.

☆　☆　☆

That is something we all long for. The question remains, however, whether we will see revivals like this in Europe in the near future. My answer is a very definite 'Yes'.

I believe God is going to do do something new and exciting on this continent. I believe that millions of people will enter into a personal relationship with God through the Lord Jesus Christ. Because of this, structures and societies will change drastically. We will see the kind of changes that took place during the time of King Josiah's reign, first century Christianity and the Welsh revival. We will see many changes for good, even though Satan will remain king of this age. We can expect him to fight back — as he did through the businessmen in Ephesus — and therefore a revival, even though it may touch millions of lives, will still be limited.

But there is more hope.

Hope for a perfect future

When we meet the Lord Jesus Christ as our personal Saviour we become a new creation; the old has gone, the new has come. We walk with the Lord and experience fellowship with Him on a daily basis. We can know what it is to have an abundant Christian life even though it will not be perfect, and will be mixed with sin, pain and sorrow. But there is a very bright future ahead. The best is yet to come. Our destination is a never-ending life in the presence of the Lord. That will be a truly perfect life — without frustrations and problems, without sin and tears, without pain and loneliness. It will be the ultimate life with the One we love so much.

So for us as individuals, the future looks very good. What about the nations? The Word of God gives us great hope for change. We should pray for and work towards the creation of a society that will honour the Lord and express His life and character. Here, too, there will be limits. Whatever good we achieve in our nations will always be mingled with sin and problems and frustrations. The work of our hands will never be perfect. But there is a bright future ahead for the world. A new order will be established where Christ will reign forever. There will be a new heaven and a new earth without Satan and the devastating results of sin. The Bible speaks very clearly about this perfect future.

When all this will come about, how it will happen and what it will be like, we do not know. But we do know from the Bible that it will come:

☆ ☆ ☆

I saw a new heaven and a new earth, for the first heaven and the first earth had passed away, and there was no longer any sea. I saw the Holy City, the New Jerusalem, coming down out of heaven from God, prepared as a bride beautifully dressed for her husband. And I heard a loud voice from the throne saying: 'Now the dwelling of God is with men, and He will live with them. They will be His people and God Himself will be with them and be their God. He will wipe away every tear from their eyes. There will be no more death or mourning or crying or pain, for the old order of things has passed away.' . . .

No longer will there be any curse. The throne of God and of the Lamb will be in the city, and His servants will serve Him. They will see His face, and His name will be on their foreheads. There will be no more night. They will not need the light of a lamp or the light of the sun, for the Lord God will give them light. And they will reign for ever and ever.

'Behold I am coming soon! My reward is with me, and I will give to everyone according to what he has done. I am the Alpha and the Omega, the First and the Last, the Beginning and the End. Blessed are those who wash their robes, that they may have the right to the tree of life and may go through the gates into the city.'

The Spirit and the bride say: 'Come!' and let him who hears say 'Come!' Whoever is thirsty, let him come; and whoever wishes, let him take the free gift of the water of life.

'Yes, I am coming soon.'

Amen. Come, Lord Jesus. (Revelation 21:1-4, 22:3-5, 12-14, 17, 20)

✩ ✩ ✩

Chapter 6

What about results?

After all that has been said about vision, 'There is Hope' campaigns and its message, it is fair to address the question of results.

Is a campaign like this worth all the energy, time and money? Have lives been changed?

What impact have these campaigns had on the different countries? Have we seen revival as a result of these campaigns?

These questions are not easy to answer, partly because the outcome of the campaigns has been quite different. Also the expectations have varied.

For instance, Myles Wilson, director of 'Project Hope' in Northern Ireland wrote:

☆　☆　☆

The problems of unemployment, violence and polarization have actually increased since we had the campaign. But even if these symptoms changed, it would not bring real hope. Hope is not dependent on circumstances; it comes through knowing and trusting the Saviour. I am saddened that circumstances have deteriorated. I am even sadder when I read the comments of a minister who explained why his church had not made any use of the Hope theme: "Having over recent years tried to in- terest the congregation in activities other than

Sunday service and being discouraged, I did not have the courage to introduce 'There is Hope'."

☆   ☆   ☆

However Swiss Christians saw direct and tangible results in their society, according to Hanspeter Nüesch, director of 'Aktion Neues Leben':

☆   ☆   ☆

Most interesting are the social effects of 'Aktion Neues Leben'. One example: the terrible youth-riots ceased both in Basel as well as in Zurich with the beginning of the prayer and evangelism outreaches. After the campaign in the area of Zurich pornography was forbidden and many sex-cinemas have been closed. The crime-rates began to drop for the first time since the Second World War and five years later they are still dropping, with the exception of the crimes related to drugs. The number of drug-addicts still grows and forms a great challenge to the Christian world in Switzerland.

☆   ☆   ☆

David Hill, chairman of 'There is Hope' Edinburgh, commented after the first campaign:

☆   ☆   ☆

Some churches have seen wonderful things happen. Others not so. The interesting thing is this: 'There is Hope' has not yet been what we have been praying for. It was good, but this was not it. It was a start and we need to continue. It was an encouraging start, but it was only modest. Many of the churches involved want to do more. The steering committee has been meeting again to pray and lay plans for an expanded project in the future. We will be asking God to lead us further along the path on which we have started.

✶ ✶ ✶

Personally I was quite disappointed after our nationwide outreach in the Netherlands. Not because nothing had happened. God had worked in a beautiful way and thousands of lives had been touched by the Gospel. However, I was disappointed because my expectations had been much higher. I had hoped and prayed for a revival in the Netherlands; a spiritual awakening that would turn the country upside down. This did not happen, or at least not yet. Because, as we will see later, 'There is Hope' has become an ongoing movement in the Netherlands. A movement that I believe will be used by God to bring a dramatic change in the Netherlands.

In studying the reports of many different evangelistic campaigns I have noted and seen the following tangible results.

1   A new vision among Christians

This is what I like to call the result of obedience. If Christians step out in faith and start proclaiming the Gospel, the first benefit is for those individual Christians and the churches to which they belong. Many Christians in the various campaigns all over Europe became actively involved in evangelism for the first time in their lives. And because of that simple fact, many of those Christians have new vision of what God can do in and through them. Countless numbers of Christians have rededicated their lives to the Lord. One minister in Belfast reported that members of his church were sustained during a period of great tension and depression in their community by the emphasis on the hope in Christ.

In Spain, José Monells reports:

☆　☆　☆

One of the most visible results came at the end of the campaign when we held a day of praise and thanksgiving to God. This was held in the Catalonian Music Hall, which was filled with about 2,500 joyful Christians. They joined together to praise the Lord and rejoice in the effort that had united us to testify for Jesus Christ.

And the movement is still going on. Many Christians who participated in the outreach, or who came to Christ during the campaign, are now serving the Lord in positions of leadership in the church. they continue to witness for our Lord Jesus Christ in Spain.

☆　☆　☆

2. *The image of churches changed*

The image the churches had in the media was often greatly influenced by the campaigns. The church used modern means and methods to communicate its old, unchanged message. This often gave a new feature to the old fashioned profile of the church. In Finland people responded upon answering the telephone by saying:

☆　☆　☆

'Finally, the church is doing something. I have been a church member all my life and this is the first time the church has come to me.'

3. Churches grew in numbers

Hanspeter Nüesch reports about Switzerland:

☆   ☆   ☆

Innumerable churches reported church growth in one way or another. This church growth was as much a qualitative growth as a quantitative one. Another interesting fact: about one-third of the volunteer workers were not engaged in church activities in any way before the campaign. After the campaign most churches received new co-workers for different kinds of activities.

☆   ☆   ☆

One Swedish pastor went to Switzerland to attend a vision conference for a saturation campaign. Back in Sweden he decided to hold his own mini-campaign. He implemented many of the lessons he had learned in Switzerland. As a result of all that his small congregation of about 50 people grew in less than one year to a weekly church attendance of over 150 people.

4. Churches learned to work together

In the Netherlands, hundreds of churches worked together as never before. In more than 250 cities, towns and villages, inter-denominational committees were formed. In many cases this was the first time ever that local churches had linked up for an evangelistic project. Now, several years later, a good percentage of these inter-church committees are still working. One of the visible results of the 'There is Hope' campaign is that churches have learned to work together.

The same is true for Northern Ireland, where 300 churches participated in the outreach; Edinburgh with 70 churches; Finland with 200 churches; and Switzerland where over 750 churches have thus far linked arms in a massive proclamation of the Gospel. This simple fact of co-operation in itself is a tremendous result of city-wide or nationwide evangelistic campaigns. Unity among Christians then becomes the powerful evangelistic vehicle that God wanted it to be. (John 17:21)

5. Millions heard the Good News

In Northern Ireland, Scotland, Spain, Portugal, Switzerland, Finland and the Netherlands literally millions of people have heard, read or seen the Good News through magazines, radio, television, films, telephone calls, large meetings, and many different church activities. It is even impossible to guess how many people have been touched in one way or another by these outreaches and how many have come closer to God because of these united evangelistic efforts.

6. Many accepted the Lord Jesus Christ as their personal Saviour

Some time ago a Swiss man approached me in the plane from Zurich to London. Even though we had never met before he recognized my face from a picture in a magazine. He then told me that he had met the Lord Jesus as his personal Saviour during a campaign in Switzerland. On my travels throughout Europe I am frequently introduced to people who have become Christians through one of these or similar evangelistic campaigns. Often I ask myself the question: 'What is a person's life worth?' And just as often I conclude that if only for this person alone, then it was worth it. But, of course, many more have found Jesus Christ as their personal Saviour. Only God knows what really happens. Some day, when we are allowed to enter into the presence of the Lord, we will see the real fruit of our labour. I am convinced that it is much more than we dare to dream.

7. *The movement continues*

After the campaign in Finland a new missionary vision was seen in local churches organizing large outreaches as a follow-up and continuation. Cities like Turku, Vaasa, Forssa, Raake, Riihimaki, Kerava and Helsinki have had various kinds of campaigns. In the capital city of Helsinki alone, there have been three large campaigns since, that have continued to draw people into the churches.

In Edinburgh, 10 churches participated in the first year in the 'There is Hope' campaign. In the second year the number increased to 30 churches. In the third year there were 50 churches. The fourth year saw the campaign increase to 10 towns and cities involving over 100 churches. At the time of going to press the movement is beginning its fifth year.

In the Netherlands we had only planned a three-month campaign. The outcome however was far beyond our expectations. After the project was officially over, the movement went on. Churches continued to organize 'Hope' outreaches, resulting in a great demand for a second magazine. So in due course, we published another magazine. This time the magazine was not distributed to every household but was sold to churches to use in their own outreach projects.

More than 750,000 copies of this second magazine were sold. The next year we published a third magazine, and later on several regional evangelistic papers.

Through these and several other experiences, we have learned that 'There is Hope' should not be seen as a single project, but rather as the beginning of a process. Evangelism is an ongoing responsibility for the church and needs careful development. Initially some churches may not be able to consider more than a single project. But those responsible for the leadership of 'There is Hope' in an area should be committed to regular, probably annual, united thrusts of evangelism under the Hope banner.

This allows the churches to develop and grow as their experience of evangelism widens, and to progressively involve more of their members in personal witnessing. It allows the number of churches involved to increase with time as they see the results of previous years' campaigns and catch a vision for themselves. It allows 'teething troubles' to be worked out. And, most importantly of all, it keeps the churches doing what they should be doing. Besides this, it should be recognized that people often need to hear the Gospel several times before being ready to respond.

A final thought on results

These then are some of the fruits Christians and churches all over Europe have seen as a result of evangelistic campaigns. Yet I still want to add a few general comments to 'results' or 'success' in Christian work.

Christian work is not dependent on results or success. the value of what we do for the Lord is not measured primarily by its outcome, but by our obedience to what He has given us to do. Of course, it is always important to work in the best possible way to reach the maximum number of people, and give ourselves fully to the task.

But even if we do not see fruit, the Lord's Great Commission to go and make disciples remains the same. God once ordered Ezekiel to go to Israel with a message. (Ezekiel 2 and 3) At the same time He told Ezekiel that the people would not listen to the message. But he still had to go. In just the same way, we have to be obedient to the Lord and go, even if we do not see fruit. In fact, most of the time when we are obedient we will see fruit, sometimes far more than we ever expected.

Also, we must remember that it is absolutely impossible to measure what has happened spiritually as a result of evangelistic work. How do you measure what the Holy Spirit has done in a person's life? How do you count the number of people who have been touched in one way or another by a message? How can you ever calculate how many people have come closer to God or accepted the Lord Jesus Christ as their personal Saviour? There is absolutely no way of finding out. And there is no need for us to know. In a sense, it is none of our business. The 'results' are simply between God and every individual.

Of course, all this does not mean that we cannot or should not evaluate an evangelistic campaign in general terms. It is also important to try to find the people who have committed their lives to the Lord so we can help them grow in their faith. But you simply cannot measure spiritual work in numbers and statistics alone. Only God knows what has really happened.

Chapter 7

What about you?

If you have read this book through to this last chapter, I take it that in one way or another it has interested or challenged you. Maybe you feel like one of the four lepers who discovered the living bread and who knows that it is sin to remain silent. Perhaps you find yourself burdened by the spiritual and social decline of Western Europe and challenged by the examples of people who took great steps of faith to proclaim the Gospel's message of hope to their societies. I hope that you, too, want to take Christ's commission seriously, to go and share the good news with the people around you.

But the question is, what are you going to do about it? How are you going to turn your conviction into action?

Let me share four practical ways in which you can be actively involved in helping to fulfil the Great Commission in your area, your country, or even in Europe.

Pray

There is a fantastic, but often untapped power in prayer. Jesus said: 'You may ask Me for anything in My name and I will do it'. (John 14:14) The apostle John wrote: 'This is the assurance we have in approaching God: that if we ask anything according to His will, He hears us. And if we know that He hears us — whatever we ask — we know that we have what we asked of Him.' (I John 5:14,15)

These are very powerful promises about prayer. The key, however, to answered prayer is 'praying in Jesus' name', or, as John puts it, 'praying according to God's will'. Of course we will not always know God's specific will immediately. It sometimes takes a while for God to get through to us by His Word or by the work of the Holy Spirit in our lives. But we can be sure of one thing: evangelism *is* according to His will. God not only desires us to be involved in spreading the good news, He commands us to do so. This fact is a foundation for great confidence when we pray for the spreading of the Gospel in our village, town, city or country. Evangelism is according to God's will and therefore He will answer our prayers. And not only that: He will often do much more than we asked for. 'Call to Me (said the Lord) and I will answer you and tell you great and unsearchable things you do not know.' (Jeremiah 33:3)

In the light of all these fantastic promises in the Bible about prayer, it is very important for us to pray daily for the spreading of the Gospel in our neighbourhood, our country and our continent. We should pray fervently for our own evangelistic efforts and for the efforts of other Christians, churches and Christian organizations. Sometimes it is hard or even impossible for us to be involved in spreading the good news ourselves, but no matter what our circumstances are we can always pray for others.

When the Amelekites attacked the Israelites during their journey through the desert (Exodus 17:18-16), Joshua and his army fought the enemy. They were in the battlefield. They had to do the work. And what did Moses, their leader, do? He went to the top of a hill with Aaron and Hur to pray. As long as Moses held up his hands, the Israelites had the upper hand in the battle. Whenever he lowered his hands, the Amalekites began to win. When Moses grew tired, Aaron and Hur supported him, so his hands remained steady until sunset. Because of the prayers of Moses and his two aides, Joshua and his army down in the valley won the battle.

It is just the same in the spiritual battle in which we are involved. We are not always fit or in the best position to participate in the battle ourselves. But we can always lift our hands up to the throne of the Lord to support the battle being fought by others. We Christians should get into the habit of praying daily for evangelism in our own sphere of influence, our country and Europe. Let's lift up our own work and the ministry of others to the throne of the Lord. Let us pray for a breakthrough for the Gospel in people's lives and in our society. Pray with confidence, because when we pray for the fulfilment of the Great Commission we know we are praying according to God's will. The Lord will surely answer when we pray for the salvation of lost souls.

Tell

A second important way in which we can be involved in helping to fulfil the Great Commission is by telling the people we meet about Jesus. And we do that not only because we have to, but also because we want to — out of love for the Lord Jesus Christ.

Remember, people are often far more interested than we expect them to be. Many people experience a spiritual vacuum in their lives, and are actually pleased to find someone interested enough in them to spend time sharing spiritual answers with them.

Take a step of faith and share with some other people the contents of the 'Knowing God Personally' booklet mentioned on page 64. Don't be disappointed if not everybody responds positively. Keep at it until you have the privilege of leading at least one person to the Lord. After that there's a good chance that you'll never stop! Seeing lives change is one of the most rewarding things a Christian can experience.

Give

There is another way you can be involved in helping to fulfil the Great Commission. No matter how much or how little we have, we can always give. God wants us to give because He wants us to benefit from sharing our possessions. There are fantastic promises in the Bible. 'Test Me in this (in giving),' says the Lord God Almighty, 'and see if I will not throw open the floodgates of heaven and pour out so much blessing that you will not have room enough for it.' (Malachi 3:10b) 'It is possible to give away and become richer.' (Proverbs 11:24, *Living Bible*) And the apostle Paul wrote to the Christians in Philippi after receiving a donation from them: 'You sent me aid again and again when I was in need. Not that I am looking for a gift, but I am looking for what may be credited to your account.' (Philippians 4:16,17)

We Christians harm ourselves and rob ourselves of the Lord's blessing if we do not give for his sake. God wants us to be distributors of His wealth; of the things He has entrusted to us in the first place.

But there is another reason why we should give. In 2 Corinthians 11:7 Paul mentions that he preached the Gospel of God free of charge to the people of Corinth. And that, of course, is the way it should be. We cannot charge non-Christians for the privilege of hearing the Gospel, even though they will benefit from it. We cannot put a price tag on the good news, even though it will cost money to share the love of Christ. And, indeed, in this modern and expensive age it costs a lot of money to take the great commission seriously. Who is going to pay?

Well, in his letter to the Christians in Corinth, Paul mentions that he 'robbed' other churches to bring the good news to them. Christians have to finance the proclamation of the Gospel. God wants us to give sacrificially so that many other people will get a chance to hear about the hope that Jesus has to offer. But do we?

I read recently in an article that we Christians spend more on pet food than on winning the lost. To my mind that is appalling. It is simply not right. We need to give as much as we can for the proclamation of the Gospel. We need to give until it hurts. We need to give sacrificially. And if we do, we will receive a double portion of joy. Firstly, we will receive special blessings from the Lord, as He promises in the Bible. But we will also have the joy of seeing people come into a living relationship with God because of our giving.

Dear brothers and sisters, if you are not already doing so, then start giving abundantly. Give to your own church, to missionary societies and Christian organizations. Commit yourself to giving as much as you can to God's work. Get involved in evangelism in your country and this continent by sharing your possessions.

Dream

Finally, dream dreams about what God can do in your neighbourhood, your city, your country. Dream dreams that only God can bring into being. Buy a map of your city or your country and hang it in your living room. Saturate yourself with the thought of reaching your society for Jesus Christ. Find other Christians whose hearts are also on fire for the Gospel. Meet with them, pray, fast, ask God what He wants you to do. Make plans about proclaiming the message of hope to every home in your area or your country. Share your vision with your church and with as many Christians as possible. Share your dreams and your enthusiasm with the leaders of your society.

And then DO SOMETHING! Step out in faith. Trust the Lord for the impossible. Share the life-giving message of hope with all the people in YOUR area, village, town, city or country.

You are important in the kingdom of God. You have a responsibility and you are needed. No matter what your circumstances are, you can always participate in the exciting challenge of the Great Commission. There is an important place for you in the army of God. You can be an ambassador of hope to your society or your country. Do not underestimate what God can do through you. His power is unlimited and the more you are open to Him the more He can do His work in and through you. You are the light of this world, so let your light shine before men. You are the salt of this society, so be an influence for good in your neighbourhood.

Dear brother or sister in the Lord, make a decision today to become involved, to do something. Commit yourself anew to the Lord and dedicate yourself to helping to fulfil Jesus' commission. Do not be afraid. God loves you. He knows you. He knows your strengths and weaknesses. Yet He wants to use you. It is His idea. He wants you to take action; to step out in faith. He will not let you down.

Commit yourself afresh into His hands with no reservations, with no holding on to any part of your own life. Allow Him to use you in any way He wants.

If this is what you want, take some time out to express your thoughts and dreams and fears to the Lord. If this is the desire of your heart, pray a prayer of commitment to the Lord and to your part in the fulfilment of the Great Commission. And why not get down on your knees for a holy moment of dedication?

'Heavenly Father, Lord Jesus, Holy Spirit, I love you.

Father I love you and thank you that you have allowed me to become your child.

Jesus I love you and thank you for all that you have done for me on the cross of Calvary.

Holy Spirit, I love you and thank you for your guidance in my life and for the power you want to give me in serving you.

Today .... I want to commit myself anew to you. I want to dedicate myself to helping fulfil your great commission. Use me in whatever way you want. Make me an ambassador of your hope in ....

Help me to pray, to share my faith, to give and to dream about what you want me to do.

Yes Lord, I am available to you.

Thank you that you want to use me for your glory.

There is hope!

Amen.'

RESPONSE CARD

Dear Leo,

Your book spoke to my heart. You challenged me
to be light and salt where I live. I want to accept
that challenge. I need help to get started. Please
tell me whom I might contact in my country that
might help me. Thank you.

Name: ....

Address: ....

....

....

Telephone: .... Age: ....

Occupation: .... Church: ....

To: Leo Habets
There is Hope
Am Zielberg
D-7840 Mullheim
West Germany

Copies of the 'Knowing God Personally' booklet
can be ordered from:
  'There is Hope'
  Campus Crusade for Christ
  Pearl Assurance House
  4 Temple Row
  Birmingham
  B2 5HG

Send s.a.e.

If you wish to receive *regular information* about *new books*, please send your name and address to:

London Bible Warehouse
PO Box 123
Basingstoke
Hants RG23 7NL

Name...

Address ....

....

....

....

I am especially interested in:
- ☐ Biographies
- ☐ Fiction
- ☐ Christian living
- ☐ Issue related books
- ☐ Academic books
- ☐ Bible study aids
- ☐ Children's books
- ☐ Music
- ☐ Other subjects